Original title:
Cosmic Rhymes and Galactic Times

Copyright © 2025 Creative Arts Management OÜ
All rights reserved.

Author: Benjamin Caldwell
ISBN HARDBACK: 978-1-80567-758-1
ISBN PAPERBACK: 978-1-80567-879-3

Celestial Configurations

In the sky, a big cheese wheel,
Asteroids dance, what a surreal feel!
Planets in pajamas, taking a stroll,
Jupiter's in slippers, feeling quite whole.

Stars play hopscotch on the Milky Way,
Venus claims she lost her way today.
Saturn's ring is quite the hula hoop,
While comets sing and make a silly troop.

Interstellar Ballad

There once was a moon with a silly face,
Who wanted to race in the vast, deep space.
With rockets made of jellybeans,
He zoomed through the stars, oh so keen!

His best friend, a comet named Elle,
Told jokes that made the universe swell.
They did flips and giggled with glee,
While aliens joined in the jubilee.

They found a black hole that swallowed a shoe,
And laughed as it spit out a bright, red view.
In a galaxy where humor shines bright,
They made every moment feel just right.

So let's sing to the stars, my friend,
In this interstellar journey, the fun won't end.
With laughter echoing through the night,
We'll travel the cosmos, what a delight!

Celestial Dance

The Milky Way throws a wacky bash,
With disco lights that shine and flash.
Planets twirl in sequined wear,
Stardust floats like glitter in the air.

A supernova plays the drums,
While Saturn shakes its ring and hums.
Orbits spin in a jolly whirl,
While asteroids around us swirl.

Galaxies twiddle their funny toes,
As we all dance in cosmic clothes.
Meteorites clap to the funky beat,
While comets groove with twinkling feet.

So grab a star and join the fun,
In this celestial soiree, everyone!
We'll prance and spin, oh what a sight!
In the universe, we dance all night!

Astral Odyssey

In a rocket made of cheese,
We zoom past Mars with ease.
Aliens wave with silly grins,
As laughter bursts and joy begins.

A comet steals my snack at night,
It zooms away, oh what a sight!
Stars giggle, planets play peek-a-boo,
Space is fun, and we will too!

Jetpacks flock like crazy ducks,
Dodging asteroids, just our luck!
We spin like tops, through light and sound,
In this wild ride, laughter's found.

So come along, let's have a blast,
In a universe that's built to last.
With every giggle, we'll take a chance,
In this silly, starry dance.

Dark Matter Dreams

Whispers of dark matter, oh so sly,
Tease the universe with a wink and a sigh.
Gravity's pulled, like a bad dad joke,
As quasars chuckle and twinkle, bespoke.

Nebulae puff out clouds of delight,
Painting the dark with colors so bright.
Superheroes in capes made of stars,
Telling tales of their interstellar wars.

Galactic Reverie

Through the void, a cat in space,
Chasing dust bunnies, oh what a race!
Saturn's rings, a hula hoop spree,
While aliens cheer on with cosmic glee.

Wormholes warp, time takes a stroll,
Einstein chuckles from his black hole.
Stars wear glasses and trade their bright light,
Making the galaxies giggle at night.

Celestial Mosaic

Bouncing moons on a cosmic trampoline,
Jupiter's storms peel off its sheen.
Silly aliens, with jellybean hats,
Debate the best flavors of galactic spats.

Shooting stars with a wink and a smile,
Zooming past in blink-worthy style.
Supernovae burst, confetti galore,
While black holes snack, always wanting more.

Infinity's Interlude

In a universe full of jest,
Stars play tag, who's the best?
Asteroids with topsy-turvy spins,
Dance with laughter, nobody wins.

Planets giggle, wobbling fast,
While comets soar and outlast.
Neptune's hiccup is quite the show,
Only Martians seem to know.

Celestial Fragments and Lunar Lullabies

Lunar lullabies echo, soft as a sneeze,
While stardust tickles the tips of your knees.
A galaxy giggles, with stars full of jest,
Spinning tales of nonsense, and never a rest.

Planets exchange puns, like balloons at a fair,
As quasars burst out like snorts in the air.
Cosmic clowns juggle, with dark matter pies,
And comets toast marshmallows, under glowing skies.

Tales from the Ether's Embrace

Floating through ether, with a giggle and cheer,
Aliens swap jokes over cups of cold beer.
Martians in capes, fly a kite made of cheese,
While Venusian ducks quack, and aim for the breeze.

Spaceships do cartwheels, with zero-gravity flair,
Jokes about gravity, they toss in the air.
Saturn's rings jingle, like silver bells sing,
As the cosmos erupts in a flash mob of bling.

Nebula Nightfall Serenade

In a whirl of colors, the horizon spins,
Nebulae wink shyly, where the laughter begins.
Stars in their pajamas, oh what a sight,
Both twinkling and chuckling, all through the night.

Meteor showers shower soggy pizza pies,
While rockets play tag in a game that defies.
Wormholes hum tunes, off-key and absurd,
As spacetime tickles, not a single word.

Echoes of the Celestial Dance

Stars twirl in pairs, like a clumsy waltz,
Planets bumping gently, oh what a jolt!
Asteroids roll past, in a playful spree,
Comets sneak glances, like kids, full of glee.

Space cows munch stardust, quite the delight,
While moon rabbits hop under sparkling light.
Galaxies giggle, and give a loud cheer,
As black holes spin tales, while sipping on beer.

Cosmic Constellation

A bear was seen in the night sky,
Eating honey, oh my oh my!
Orion waved his sword around,
While Draco just crawled on the ground.

Stars are gossiping, what a scene,
About planets who wear too much green.
If black holes had ears, they'd surely hear,
All the secrets we hold dear.

Chronicles of the Cosmos

Once a rocket dreamed so tall,
To catch a star, it took a fall.
It landed soft on Mars' red sheet,
And shouted, 'Fried eggs would be a treat!'

Neptune giggled in the dark,
As comets whizzed with a spark.
They claimed to be the fastest guys,
But really, just great at silly lies.

Universe in Verse

The moon tried to sing a tune,
But forgot the words, oh what a boon!
The sun just laughed, and shone so bright,
Said, 'Try again, you'll get it right!'

Planets spin in a merry race,
Venus wants a little space.
Mercury speeds, saying, 'What's the rush?'
While Earth is stuck in a traffic hush.

Pulsar Prose

A star twinkles in the sky,
It wonders what's for lunch, oh my!
Is it a comet? Or some fries?
Its sauce is written in the sighs.

Jupiter dances with a gleeful spin,
While Saturn's rings clap, a cosmic din.
Mars is grumpy, it wants some cake,
But all it gets is a meteor shake.

Ethereal Rhapsody

A comet winks in a twinkling dance,
While solar flares give aliens romance.
Asteroid burgers sizzling bright,
As meteors eat them with delight.

Stars hold court in a nebula's glow,
Laughing so loud, they put on a show.
With jokes about gravity and its quirks,
The universe chuckles, and time just smirks.

Enigmas of the Ether

Why do meteors wear such bright hats?
And aliens dance with garden rats?
Planets blow bubbles, floating with glee,
While asteroids shout, 'Look! There's a bee!'

Galaxies trade secrets in the night,
'What's your favorite snack?' 'Oh, starlight bite!'
Quasars wink at the Milky crew,
Saying, 'Bet you can't guess what we'll do!'

Stories Written in Starlight

Once a moon cat grinned wide,
Painted galaxies with cosmic pride.
A star said, 'Hey, watch me float!'
As rockets wore their best coat.

Uranus laughed, spinning like mad,
While black holes played peek-a-boo, oh, so glad!
Nebulae giggled, weaving their yarn,
A tapestry of mischief on a cosmic farm.

Constellation Dreams

Stars gather like a big, bright crew,
To share tales of the things they do.
A bear and a lion, in a playful fight,
Chasing each other through the night.

Orion trips over his own two feet,
As Pleiades giggles, can't take the heat.
They paint the sky with laughter's glow,
In dreams of starlight, where fun will flow.

The North Star points out funny sights,
Like aliens grilling on moonlit nights.
With winks and nods, the cosmos scheme,
In this vast playground of silly dreams.

So wish upon a star tonight,
Join the dance, there's pure delight.
In the fabric of space, where joy beams,
Come weave your wishes in constellation dreams.

Galactic Gazette

In the skies where aliens play,
UFOs zooming, bright and gay.
One lost a shoe while dancing low,
Now they all wear mismatched glow.

Jupiter's moons throw a wild bash,
Saturn's rings like a cosmic sash.
Martians sip on fizzy pop,
As comets crash and asteroids hop.

Stars gossip about their shine,
Pleading for some extra wine.
Nebulas swirl in a silly dance,
While black holes sing and prance by chance.

So grab your rockets, join the fun,
Where stellar laughs weigh a ton.
In our galaxy's big community,
Laughter's the real opportunity.

Planetary Verses

Venus threw a tea party last night,
The cakes were shaped just like a flight.
Mercury tried to bake a star,
But it melted, causing quite the spar.

Mars wore a hat made of red dust,
Claimed it was chic, a galactic must.
Asteroids rolled in just for kicks,
Cracking jokes about space tricks.

Neptune juggled moons with flair,
While Saturn giggled without a care.
Uranus snorted soda through rings,
Oh, the joy that laughter brings!

Pluto sneezed, a starry blast,
Still, it's here, we love it fast.
In this universe so vast and bright,
Laughter echoes across the night.

Twilight of the Stars

In twilight zones where starlights blink,
Aliens gather for a cosmic drink.
They toast their quirks with glowing cups,
With jokes that make the nebula erupt.

A supernova tried to rap,
But tripped on light, fell in a flap.
The milky way can't stop the cheer,
For every burst, there's laughter near.

Galactic jesters dance on beams,
With moonlit hopes and starry dreams.
Black holes chuckle at all the fuss,
While shooting stars make wishes thus.

When the sun yawns at the end of day,
And wishes the moon to come out and play,
It's just a game of silly rhymes,
In the laughter of the endless times.

Celestial Navigations

Navigators of the sky so bright,
Charting paths with laughter in sight.
An alien with a starry map,
Got lost twice, now calls it a trap.

Pluto's dog barks at passing moons,
Thinking they're just giant balloons.
While astronauts crack jokes mid-flight,
Strapped in tight, what a silly sight!

Constellations giggle at their shapes,
Winking down at odd little drapes.
A black hole yawns, stretches wide,
And swallows a comet, what a ride!

So, grab your ships and join the race,
Across the cosmos, a funny space.
In this vast wonder, remember to rhyme,
With celestial chuckles keeping time.

Starlight Verses

In a galaxy not so far,
The stars giggle, grinning bizarre.
Planets dance with silly grace,
As comets trip in a cosmic race.

Aliens with wacky hats,
Hold interstellar chats with cats.
Black holes swirl with laughter and cheer,
As space-time hugs you, drawing near.

Nebulas puff like cotton candy,
Spreading joy that's quite dandy.
Shooting stars wink and tease,
While space worms play hopscotch with ease.

So lift your gaze to skies so wide,
Where laughter knows no bumpy ride.
In the night, the universe beams,
With starlit jokes and silly dreams.

Infinity's Cadence

In quantum states where quirks reside,
Atoms do a funny slide.
Waves jitterbug through time and space,
While photons grin in the race.

The universe plays hide and seek,
Where dark matter hides if you speak.
Galaxies spin in a dizzy whirl,
As time-loop pranks start to unfurl.

In the void, a giggle grows,
As cosmic dust sneezes and glows.
Jumping particles, a raucous game,
In a universe that's quite insane.

So let the rhythm lift your soul,
In the vastness, we all roll.
With each beat, let yourself unwind,
In this funhouse made for all to find.

The Poetry of Portals

Through portals flashy, bright and weird,
Dimension doors have all appeared.
Jumpy elves on rocket ships,
Sip stardust smoothies, take quick sips.

Planets swap their places, swap their tunes,
Dancing across the light of moons.
Wormholes laughing loud and clear,
Whisper secrets that we can't hear.

Parallel worlds with jellybean shores,
And time-traveling boots for outlandish tours.
Each verse echoes through the space,
As every quasar wears a funny face.

So leap through doors, embrace the fun,
In this wild dance of everyone.
From twilight's gleam to dawn's first sight,
The laughter of the stars is our delight.

Radiance in Reverberation

Echoes bounce in galactic halls,
With laughter ringing from cosmic walls.
Radiance tickles passing asteroids,
And quarks giggle in planetary voids.

Gravity plays a cheeky game,
As comets juggle, seeking fame.
Stars chuckle as they twinkle bright,
With every wink, they spread delight.

In this universe of countless beams,
Where silly moments burst at the seams,
Space-time wobbles, grinning wide,
As cosmic clowns dance with pride.

So join the show, let's laugh and soar,
In the vastness, forever explore.
With echoes bouncing high and free,
The universe hums a tune of glee.

Echoes in the Ether

In a galaxy not too far,
Balloons of stardust float like stars.
Aliens giggle at Earthlings' prance,
Dancing on waves of a cosmic chance.

Jokes in the vacuum travel so light,
They bounce off planets in the night.
A comet slips on its own long tail,
While meteors munch on a space-time trail.

Gravity's just a playful tease,
It pulls on your pants and makes you sneeze.
Asteroids stroll, with swagger and flair,
While black holes laugh with a swirling hair.

So next time you gaze at the bright sky's dome,
Remember the giggles of friends far from home.
Stars twinkle just to share a grin,
As laughter in the void begins to spin.

Astral Allure

In the depths of the stellar mix,
Planets play poker with silly tricks.
The Sun wears shades, so bright and bold,
While moons giggle, their secrets unfold.

A satellite woos a comet so shy,
With cheesy lines that make it fly high.
As meteors roast marshmallows on air,
They toast to the jokes that float everywhere.

Time's little clock ticks with a clumsy whirr,
Telling tales of a space-age slur.
Octopi fly on jetpacks of glee,
Trading jokes with the stars and the sea.

So dance with the galaxies, swing with delight,
Embrace the funny, from day into night.
For every chuckle that's crafted with skill,
A universe stirs, inspired by the thrill.

Timeless Universes

In distant realms where oddities bloom,
Tommy the comet claims space as his room.
He throws wild parties with stars on the run,
And aliens groove just to have a bit of fun.

Nebulas bounce to a disco beat,
Asteroids jitterbug, tapping their feet.
Space cows moo to an invisible tune,
While sunspots scuffle in a wild polka swoon.

Wormholes twist with a silly grin,
Pulling in laughter, letting the joy spin.
Galactic giggles echo through the seams,
Tickling timelines until bursting at the beams.

So let's toast to oddness, cheers through the night,
To a universe filled with silly delight.
For in every laugh that's ignited and shared,
A timeless adventure is joyfully bared.

Dance of the Distant Suns

Out in the void, where no one can hear,
Bright suns tango with a dollop of cheer.
They spin and they twirl, on gravity's stage,
With supernovae barking, "Turn up the page!"

Funky little planets join in the fray,
With hula hoops made of Saturn's rings in their play.
While Venus serves drinks in a stellar café,
Pluto just jokes about being away.

Cosmic confetti rains down from above,
As galaxies twist to the rhythm of love.
Quasars dress up and prance in their light,
Inviting all comets to join in the night.

So when starlight winks in a humorous way,
Join in the dance without delay.
In the grandest ball of the celestial spree,
Laughter is timeless, and so are we.

Celestial Choreography

Stars are dancing in the night,
Twinkling left, then bouncing right.
Planets flip in cosmic glee,
While comets giggle, 'Look at me!'

Asteroids roll like bowling balls,
While Saturn's rings just have a ball.
Neptune's blue is quite the scene,
While Mars is just a red machine.

Uranus spins with quite the flair,
A tilted twirl, with style and care.
Each nebula has jokes to tell,
In this vast space, we're under a spell!

So join the waltz of endless space,
With playful stars, let's find our place.
In this universe of lively tunes,
Even black holes hum their funny tunes!

Elysium of the Expanse

In a realm where stardust flows,
Galaxies wear their sparkly clothes.
Gravity whimsically pulls a prank,
While space-time giggles in a prank!

Planets roll like playful dice,
Jupiter sings, 'Hey, I'm not nice!'
Venus pouts with her thick, hot air,
But even she can't help but stare.

Wormholes open for a quick peek,
"A shortcut," they say, "is what you seek!"
Quasars flash like a gallery,
While shooting stars laugh, 'What a folly!'

In this grand expanse, life can delight,
With humor tucked in every night.
So float among these sparkling chimes,
And join the fun of festive times!

Orion's Overture

Orion struts with mighty pride,
While Sirius winks, twinkling wide.
Betelgeuse is a moonlit clown,
Spinning tales in a stellar gown.

The universe brings a comic show,
With black holes that swallow just for show.
Pulsars click, like a cosmic clock,
While space kitties chase the moon's stock.

Stars can't help but laugh and sing,
As comets drape their tails like bling.
Each constellation has a joke,
In this sky, the giggles provoke.

So take a seat in starlit space,
Laughter drifts with a gentle grace.
For in the night where wonders roam,
Let's chill with humor, far from home!

Whispering Galaxies

Galaxies whisper in sweet delight,
Painting the dark with colors bright.
'Hey, want to play a game of tag?'
As the stars dodge in a cosmic brag.

Planets laugh and giggle too,
'Who's got the best orbit? Me or you?'
Mercury's speed is quite the show,
But Venus rolls her eyes, 'Oh, no!'

Nebulae swirl with a colorful flair,
'We're the dessert, how's the cosmic fare?'
While shooting stars make a mess so grand,
Painting wishes in the nighttime sand.

So join the dance of the cosmic play,
Where laughter echoes light-years away.
In this universe where humor shines,
Every laugh is a jewel that aligns!

Celestial Bodies and Silvery Songs

The moon's a cheese and stars are sprinkles,
Comets zoom by with squeaky tinkles.
Planets dance in circles slow,
While aliens sing tunes from long ago.

A star once tripped on its own light beam,
Fell into a black hole, oh what a scream!
The sun just laughed, a jolly big guy,
As meteorites raced like popcorn on high.

Venus wears shades, looking quite sly,
While Mars quips, 'I'm the red guy!'
Galaxies swirl in a cosmic ballet,
And asteroids groove in their own way.

So let's toast to the universe's charms,
With punch made from stardust and cosmic arms.
Laughter rings out across the vast space,
As stars wink mischievously, a gleeful chase.

Starlit Pathways and Galactic Fables

On a starlit path, the fairies all glide,
With jokes that make even black holes wide.
Saturn's rings go bling in bright hues,
While space mice dance in their shiny shoes.

A comet tried juggling some planets one day,
But tripped and sent Mars flying away.
Venus just chuckles, sipping her tea,
While Jupiter blusters, 'Not funny to me!'

Tales of adventures in the Milky Way,
Where aliens sneak in to join the fray.
They bring silly hats and a can of space soda,
Creating wild parties as they dance a cha-cha.

So grab your rocket and come take a ride,
In the fun-filled space where laughter won't hide.
Together we'll spin through the cosmic delight,
Finding humor in darkness, and joy in the night.

The Poetry of Black Holes and Bright Sparks

Black holes whisper with a witty spin,
As bright sparks giggle, let the fun begin!
A neutron star struts in a celestial coat,
While supernovae ponder, 'Did we just gloat?'

Quasars flash bright, but can't find their socks,
While folding space into funny, absurd blocks.
Galaxies collide with a laugh and a bump,
Leaving stardust trails, all crazy and plump.

A starfish in space thinks he's quite a hit,
With arms going wild, he refuses to sit.
And what about Pluto? The underdog claims,
"Don't forget my name; I'm still in the games!"

So let's celebrate all the quirks out there,
In the wackiest theater of cosmic flair.
With laughter and light, we take to the skies,
In this universe where humor never dies.

Stardust Dreams and Celestial Schemes

In stardust dreams where giggles abound,
Planets plot pranks all around.
A galaxy spins with a silly old grin,
While meteors zoom with a playful spin.

Aliens concoct their favorite dish,
It's green and gooey, but oh, what a wish!
Saturn just juggles its moons in a game,
While Venus insists, 'Don't forget my name!'

The sun tells jokes that light up the night,
While stars exchange winks with a twinkling delight.
A black hole winks, "I'm the perfect tease!"
Swallowing space-burgers with cosmic ease.

So let's dance among constellations so bright,
With laughter that twinkles all the way to the night.
In the grandeur of space, let silliness reign,
As we sip on our stardust, feeling no pain.

Threads of Infinity in Night's Veil

In a world where stars wear hats,
Galaxies hide from dancing cats.
The planets spin in a wobbly way,
While astronauts sip on milky spray.

Comets laugh as they zoom by fast,
Making wishes, oh what a blast!
Nebulas twirl in their glittery gowns,
Creating chaos, spinning round towns.

Aliens whisper through the void,
Finding humor in asteroids destroyed.
Each twinkle carries a cheeky grin,
As space critters play, let the fun begin!

So gaze at the night with a chuckle and cheer,
For the universe knows how to persevere.
It's a merry show, far and wide,
Where the threads of infinity become our guide.

The Dance of Light and Darkness

Light winks at shadows, what a sight,
While darkness hopes to steal the light.
Stars wear disco balls on their heads,
And the moon just giggles as it spreads.

The sun and moon skip across the sky,
Trading secrets with a wink and a sigh.
As twilight bursts into a happy tune,
It's a dance-off party with the sun and moon!

Planets bounce, they can't get enough,
Painting the universe, oh how fun and tough!
A black hole chuckles, eating stars in sight,
While meteors tumble, adding to the light.

So hold on tight in this grand ballet,
Where each twinkle makes worries sway.
In this jitterbug of dark and gleam,
There's laughter echoing in every dream.

Messages in the Cosmic Breeze

Whispers travel on starlit winds,
Sending secrets where laughter begins.
An asteroid grins, sending out a tune,
While space dust dances beneath the moon.

Galaxies giggle in playful spins,
As supernovas burst, they surely win.
The Milky Way plays hopscotch with light,
Each twinkling star shares a joke on its flight.

A cosmic postcard floats through the night,
Reading 'Greetings from Pluto, it's outta sight!'
With comets writing stories in their trails,
Each tale a chuckle that never fails.

So listen close in the stillness of space,
For funny messages float without a trace.
In every breeze is a quirky twist,
A symphony of laughter that can't be missed.

Chasing Comets, Catching Dreams

Chasing comets with a silly grin,
Hoping to catch them, oh where to begin?
They zoom right past, teasing with flair,
Like trying to hug the cold night air.

Dreams ride on those comet tails,
Sailing through stardust, leaving trails.
A rocket laughs at its own silly song,
While planets groove and hum along.

With each blink, a wish takes flight,
As shooting stars paint the sky so bright.
The universe chuckles, 'What a dream!'
As we fling our hopes in a cosmic beam.

So grab that dream, don't let it fade,
Dance with the comets, ain't it a trade?
For in laughter, we find our gleam,
Chasing comets and catching dreams.

The Color of the Cosmos

In a nebula of neon hues,
Stars are wearing fancy shoes.
Jupiter's got a paint job new,
While Saturn's rings are stripes of blue.

Mars is blushing, looks quite shy,
Venus thinks she's the butterfly.
Pluto's feeling left out today,
He just wants a cosmic play!

Neptune's throwing a color bash,
With comets zooming in a flash.
Uranus sings a silly tune,
While asteroids dance 'neath the moon.

Gravity's got a wobbly twist,
In the universe, we can't resist.
Laughing stars and giggling suns,
Join the party; everyone runs!

Arcane Adventures in the Void

Through the void, we drift and glide,
On a spaceship made from a pizza pie.
Alien pals, they crack us up,
With a joke about a plucky cup!

Black holes twist like rubber bands,
While stardust tickles space-faring hands.
Galactic giggles echo loud,
As we soar above the starry crowd.

Hyperdrive makes us fly like fish,
Wishing for an interstellar dish.
Snack time on the Milky Way route,
Eating space fries with no doubt!

Soaring past a cosmic mall,
Where aliens buy and sell it all.
We barter jokes instead of gold,
For laughter's worth is more than told!

Luminous Rhythms

The universe drops a funky beat,
As meteors dance on their little feet.
Planets swing in a galactic groove,
While comets spin—it's time to move!

Dancing suns with their fiery flair,
Remind us not to comb our hair.
While stars wink with a sparkly eye,
They sashay across the velvet sky!

Asteroids play a jazzy tune,
Making music with the craters' swoon.
Quasars humming a swingy sound,
In this rhythmic playground we've found!

Black holes sway with a graceful flair,
Pulling us in without a care.
In this cosmic rave, we all unite,
Jamming together both day and night!

Cosmic Secrets in Starlight

In starlit skies, secrets abound,
Like why aliens don't wear a crown.
Whispers travel on solar wind,
Tales of mischief the skies rescind.

A UFO lost its way home,
Now it roams through the Milky Dome.
Aliens giggling, plotting their pranks,
While black holes hide behind their ranks.

Orion's belt, a fashion blunder,
With stars that sparkle like cotton candy thunder.
Pleiades laughs, "What's your style?"
And Venus yells, "Stay back a while!"

Eclipses play their favorite game,
Hiding moons, bringing stars to fame.
In the night sky, mysteries shine,
With cosmic laughter, we're all entwined!

Lightyear Lyrics

In a rocket ship made of cheese,
We zoom past stars with silly ease.
Martians dance in sparkly hats,
While aliens juggle furry rats.

Planets shout with giggly glee,
As we sip on moonlit tea.
Jupiter's got a prancing tune,
A waltz beneath a shiny moon.

Asteroids clink like silverware,
Bumping into things mid-air.
Saturn's rings play peek-a-boo,
As we laugh, oh what a view!

With comets zipping all around,
We sing and make the silliest sound.
In this space where time will freeze,
Let's just roll in stardust sneeze!

Aurora's Embrace

Dancing lights across the sky,
A rainbow wave that makes us sigh.
The sun plays tricks while stars are bright,
As night giggles in pure delight.

Whispers swirl in colors bold,
Stories of the brave and old.
But here we sit with popcorn fun,
Watching auroras dance and run.

Frogs in space sport vibrant hues,
Trading tales in sparkly shoes.
With every twirl and every flip,
We're stuck in joy's eternal grip.

So let the beams tickle your nose,
As we snooze where the starlight glows.
With shots of laughter, we will cheer,
In this embrace, there's nothing to fear!

Celestial Musings

Planets have their own parade,
With marching stars that serenade.
The Milky Way sings silly tunes,
While asteroids wear hats like loons.

Galaxies spin like cotton candy,
And space is always quite dandy.
Supernovae laugh and play,
As comets zoom and gleefully sway.

Uranus plays hide and seek,
While black holes sip on cosmic leak.
Laughter echoes in the void,
Where humor and wonder are enjoyed.

So let's gather round, my friend,
In this scene where giggles blend.
With every twinkle in the night,
Spaceship joy takes off in flight!

Fragments of Eternity

Stardust sneezed and flew away,
As time forgot to play today.
We chased after a playful wink,
In a galaxy of lemonade pink.

Nebulas throw a glitter bash,
Making rain clouds from cosmic trash.
Dancing meteors leap and spin,
While astronauts wear cheeky grins.

Time ticks backwards, what a treat!
As we trip over our own feet.
Stars drop jokes like falling spice,
Creating giggles that feel so nice.

So gather up those twinkling dreams,
And let the universe burst at the seams.
In fragments of this endless play,
We'll laugh together all the way!

Twilight of the Infinite

In a galaxy far, quite unknown,
A comet tripped over a cosmic bone.
Stars giggled and danced in the light,
While aliens played hopscotch all night.

Planets wore hats made of cheese,
As meteors sailed with the greatest of ease.
Black holes burped, and worlds gave a cheer,
"What a ruckus!" said Space, "I love it here!"

Every moon winked at the sun's warm smile,
And gravity joined in, lightening the style.
Asteroids juggled with a flair
While rockets laughed at the weight of air.

So the twilight spun in a quirky delight,
Painting the cosmos with colors so bright.
Laughter echoed through the nebulous gaps,
As stellar beings enjoyed their cosmic naps.

Starborn Serenities

In a nebula swirl, on a cloud made of fluff,
The stars crack jokes and it's never too tough.
Supernovas pop like confetti in space,
While time ticks on with a comical face.

Saturn spins rings with an air of disdain,
"Why can't you see? I'm not spins, I'm chains!"
Mars rolls its eyes, seeking moments of peace,
While Venus just giggles, "Oh, give me some fleece!"

Comets race by, dressed up in bling,
With tails that flutter like a celestial wing.
The Milky Way shimmies, a grand cosmic dance,
Where laughter erupts at each gala's expanse.

Each twinkling star has a silly pun,
Making the dark fun, oh what a run!
With every wink of the moon so keen,
The universe bursts out, 'We're here to be seen!'

Starlit Whispers of the Universe

On a starlit night, the skies came alive,
A gassy giggle made the comets thrive.
Nebulas whispered their secrets in jest,
While space dust sparkled, feeling quite blessed.

Jupiter challenged the moons to a race,
While Venus just laughed, floating free in her space.
Saturn sighed, "These rings are a bore,"
But they twirled and twirled—who could ask for more?

Uranus cracked jokes that made others blush,
Near the cosmic fountain, there was quite a hush.
Starlight collided, creating a brawl,
Galactic humor echoed, together through all.

Lightyears away, where laughter knows no bounds,
Galaxies swirl in these joyous sounds.
The fabric of space gave a jubilant cheer,
As the universe smiled, finally clear.

Celestial Melodies in the Void

In the vacuum, where silence is bold,
Planetary pranks began to unfold.
A black hole strummed on a void-shaped guitar,
While quasars hummed tunes from afar.

Eclipses played peek-a-boo with the sun,
As meteors raced, just for fun.
Stars crooned softly, serenades to the night,
While rays of light twinkled, oh what a sight!

Galaxies spun like ballerinas in jest,
In an interstellar flash mob, they felt so blessed.
Asteroids, dressed in their grooviest threads,
Joined the dance floor, where no one treads.

As the night turned to day, laughter did stay,
The universe chuckled in a beautiful way.
For in this grand tapestry, humor entwined,
Brought joy to the void, endlessly kind.

The Language of Stars

The stars giggle in the night,
Whispering tales of pure delight.
They dance around in twinkling chat,
Winking at us, how about that?

Planets blush with each comet's kiss,
As meteors laugh, what a hit or miss!
Asteroids play hopscotch on a whim,
Whilst solar winds hum a happy hymn.

Galaxies swirl in a cosmic hug,
Nebulas puff like a fluffy rug.
They make wishes, they make jokes,
Stardust laughter, what a hoax!

So when you gaze at the night so bright,
Remember the giggles that sparkle in sight.
The universe jesting in a dazzling glow,
A comedic performance, don't you know?

Time Between the Worlds

In the pause between seconds we play,
With time travelers having a fun day.
They trip over clocks, oh what a sight,
Silly antics in the fluttering light.

One jumps ahead, another falls back,
Time gets confused, we're on the wrong track.
They argue on minutes; who counts for fun?
'Every tick is a dance!' a chrono-bun.

In the middle of ages, they sip tea,
Discussing the future and what could be.
In parallel realms, they tell wild tales,
Of dinosaurs going on moonlit trails.

So here we spin in time's friendly laughter,
Moments collide, they chase after.
As seconds giggle and minutes chime,
Who knew we had so much time to rhyme?

Echoes of Tomorrow

Tomorrow echoes with silly sound,
As future folks gather all around.
They trade goofy gadgets and strange new hats,
Giggling over their robot cats.

They plan to dance in neon skies,
Skipping through time, what a surprise!
Sending messages back to the past,
Shouting, "Look at us! We'll have a blast!"

With flying cars made from bubblegum,
And candy rockets that go 'boom' and 'hum'.
They leave trails of glitter, a sight to see,
While laughing through space, so wild and free.

So beware when the future does call,
It's bound to make you giggle and sprawl.
In echoes of laughter, the world spins bright,
Tomorrow's tricks keep us filled with delight!

Spheres of Solitude

In spheres of solitude, we trip and twirl,
Monkeys in spacesuits, giving it a whirl.
They swing from asteroids, an aerial scheme,
Dreaming up planets like a wild dream.

Around lonely moons, they play hide and seek,
Who amongst them can play peek-a-boo sleek?
Whimsical winks from those far-off spheres,
Chasing laughter amongst cosmic cheers.

While comets chuckle, they draw in the dust,
Twisting and turning, it's a must!
Galactic giggles reside in the mist,
As laughter in space cannot be missed.

So dance in your solitude, let joy take flight,
For amidst the stars, there's plenty of light.
With humor and glee, we glide and we roam,
Finding joy in the vastness, we make it our home!

Cosmic Cadence

In space, the pockets of stars giggle,
Planets dance and sometimes wiggle.
Comets race with a cheeky cheer,
While aliens toast with their space beer.

Asteroids zipping, quite the sight,
Dodging each other, what a flight!
Gravity's pull? They just won't budge,
Cuz they're too busy to even judge.

Saturn's rings say, 'Look at me!'
While Mars just sighs, 'Let me be free.'
Jupiter hops in a bouncy game,
Pointing and laughing, oh what a fame.

And so, the stars in their merry way,
Spin tales of fun, night and day.
In a galactic dance of pure delight,
The universe giggles, oh what a night!

Universe Unveiled

A black hole whispers a funny jest,
'Try to escape, you won't, just rest!'
Nebulas puff like a cosmic cloud,
'Get your selfies!' say stars, quite loud.

The moon pulls tides with a silly sway,
While Earth spins round, just wanting to play.
Mars talks back with a spicy flair,
Saying, 'Check out my red, beyond compare!'

Little space critters play hide and seek,
Hiding in craters, oh what a peek!
Galaxies swirl with a dizzying spin,
Creating a ruckus, laughter within.

As comets zoom with tails of glee,
The universe beams, 'Come dance with me!'
In this grand cosmic show, we find,
The brightest jokes that space can unwind.

Astral Harmonies

In the depths of night, stars hum a tune,
While Saturn jokes, 'I'm a planet, not a balloon!'
The sun winks brightly, full of sass,
'Without me, you know, it's a total pass!'

Gravity grumbles, 'Why so down?'
While asteroids giggle, spinning 'round.
Mars pulls faces, rather bold,
Saying, 'I'm precious, not just gold!'

Quasars burst with laughter so loud,
'We're the rockstars of this galactic crowd!'
Black holes spin yarns of curious tales,
While stars ride bicycles with shining trails.

There's fun in the void, if you dare to glance,
Just join in the cosmic, quirky dance.
Each twinkling wink is a joyful rhyme,
Sparking laughter through the fabric of time.

Starlit Reflections

Clouds drift by in a cosmic frolic,
Jupiter's storms can be quite melodic.
Venus winks with a dazzling show,
'Can you handle my beauty? Oh, do let it grow!'

Stardust rains like jellybean treats,
While meteors play tag in swift, funny feats.
Tiny aliens poke their heads out,
'Is it snack time yet? We have no doubt!'

The space-time rift laughs, 'Caught you there!'
As time swirls around like a hippy bear.
Antares giggles with a glimmering gleam,
'Join the party, it's a celestial dream!'

So here we flow through this wanderous spree,
In a universe filled with fun and glee.
The stars may twinkle, they may tease,
But laughter's the language that's sure to please!

A Symphony of Stars and Shadows

In the night, the stars do sing,
With twinkling lights, what joy they bring.
Yet shadows dance with comical grace,
Trip on their toes, oh what a face!

Planets laugh, each wobble's a joke,
While Saturn spins with a shiny cloak.
Mars grumbles about his rusty hue,
While Venus winks, 'Hey, I'm hotter than you!'

The comets flip, a cosmic ballet,
Shooting stars shout, 'Hey! Look our way!'
In this cosmic concert, chaos reigns,
While Uranus giggles, rubbing his chains!

Oh, what fun, as night's curtain falls,
Our universe gives one last call.
So grab your popcorn and take a seat,
For a show of giggles that's quite the treat!

Beyond the Milky Way's Dream

On a journey far from home we roam,
Past milk that's free, a celestial foam.
Aliens wave from their quirkiest ships,
While nebulae swirl in colorful dips.

A star sneezes, oh what a sight!
While moons bicker, who's bright, who's light.
With laughter echoing through the void,
We find joy where the stars have toyed.

Asteroids ponder their rocky fate,
'Are we just rubble or something great?'
With a chuckle, a dwarf planet swings,
While a supernova does a little flings!

So let's dance among the shining spheres,
With ticklish twinkles and giggling cheers.
Beyond the dreams of milky delight,
The cosmos is strange, but oh so bright!

The Language of Asteroids and Comets

Asteroids chat with a rumbling sound,
'Hey, watch it!' as they tumble around.
While comets swoosh in a flurry of light,
'Excuse my tail, I'm quite the sight!'

They share stories of gravitational wars,
And who can flip the best cosmic doors.
Though rocky and icy, there's laughter in air,
As they duel with puns of solar flare.

A meteoroid whizzes, 'I'm faster than you!'
While a comet retorts, 'But I glow like a dew!'
In this stellar ruckus, they spin and they zoom,
Creating a symphony in every room.

So when you gaze at the night's starry page,
Remember the fun of the galactic stage.
For asteroids giggle and comets do jest,
In this universe, laughter's the best!

Midnight Murmurs from the Stars

At midnight, the stars whisper in glee,
'Tell me a secret, do you see me?'
And the moon chimes in with a silvery laugh,
Saying, 'You're all bright, just look at your staff!'

Constellations gossip in twinkling tones,
Sharing their tales of long-lost drones.
Orion fakes a cough, what a funny sight,
While Pleiades giggles, spreading her light.

With each twinkle, the cosmos conspire,
Creating a tale that spirals higher.
Shooting stars make wishes on frosty nights,
While black holes yawn, saying, 'Oh, what a fright!'

So here's to the whispers from above,
An ensemble of stars, a galactic love.
So join in the laughter, oh don't be shy,
For even the universe needs a good cry!

Light and Shadow in Space

Twinkling stars with winks so bright,
They dance around in the velvet night.
But watch out for shadows, they sneak and creep,
Making space explorers lose their sleep.

Asteroids roll like bowling balls,
While space cats make their silly calls.
"Is that a planet or just my hat?"
Galactic antics, imagine that!

Comets trail like bad perfume,
As aliens dance in the cosmic room.
They juggle moons and sip stardust tea,
Aerial acrobatics, oh whee!

In the galaxy, laughter rings,
Gravity plays tricks and tugs at strings.
A game of tag 'round the Milky swirl,
Who knew space could be this whirled?

The Riddle of the Universe

What's bigger, the stars or my morning toast?
At breakfast time, I'm a galaxy host.
With jelly planets and syrupy sun,
Eating space pancakes, oh what fun!

Black holes are where my socks disappear,
In another dimension, they dance with cheer.
The cosmos giggles, a joke untold,
"Why did the star cross the sky? Be bold!"

Time wobbles like gelatin in flight,
Ticking and tocking through endless night.
"Why is a nebula so hard to explain?
Just ask a space chicken who's gone insane!"

As I ponder the universe's riddle,
A little green guy plays a space fiddle.
"Join me in fun, let's twist and shout,
In this funny cosmos, there's no doubt!"

Songs of the Milky Way

In the Milky Way, where fun never ends,
Giant space whales are singing with friends.
They splash through stardust, they leap and glide,
And swing on rings like a cosmic slide.

Dancing comets twirl with grace,
While meteors laugh in a whimsical race.
"Catch me if you can!" they shout with glee,
While black holes snicker, "Welcome to me!"

Astro-birds chirp in a joyful tune,
Sipping star juice 'neath a floating moon.
They strut their stuff in a dazzling show,
With mic-asteroids stealing the glow!

So join the melody, let your heart sway,
With laughter and music, we'll brighten the day.
In this starry disco, let's sing and play,
For the universe jams in a spectacular way!

Transcendental Tides

Waves of starlight crash on the shore,
As space surfers ride cosmic lore.
With neon boards and galactic flair,
They shout, "Hang ten in the starlight air!"

The moon pulls tides like a cosmic prank,
While suns share jokes that draw a blank.
"Why did the photon break up with the wave?
It found a new partner, so suave, so braves!"

Galaxies swirl like a swirling drink,
While space porpoises giggle and wink.
They leap through nebulae, what a sight,
With bursts of delight in the cool starlight.

So come ride the tides of a universe mad,
Full of funny moments and laughs that we've had.
In the realm of the stars, let our spirits glide,
On the waves of wonder, let joy be our guide.

Harmonics of the Infinite Sky

Twinkling stars dance in a line,
They wear their sparkles, oh so fine.
One says, 'I'm a superstar!'
The others chuckle, 'You're bizarre!'

Planets spin like tops gone wild,
Each one's a cosmic, playful child.
They giggle as they whirl around,
In the silence, laughter's found.

A comet zooms with ice cream dreams,
Leaving trails of whipped cream beams.
"Catch me if you can!" it cries,
Through nebulae it swiftly flies.

In the orbit where pulsars beat,
Martians throw a disco feat.
With beeping lights and funky tunes,
Jiving under playful moons.

The Rhythm of Planets in Motion

Mercury skips in speedy haste,
Venus twirls in a fragrant paste.
Earth waves as it spins just right,
'Hey there, Moon! Come dance tonight!'

Jupiter jumps, oh what a sight,
With swirling storms as its delight.
Saturn brings the rings to swing,
While Uranus laughs at everything.

Neptune hums a dreamy tune,
Pluto pops in with a balloon.
They all join in a galactic jam,
Counting stars, oh what a spam!

Even black holes can't resist,
They try to join but just can't twist.
In this waltz of the sky's embrace,
Every wobble holds its place.

Solar Serenades and Stellar Stories

The sun sings loud, a bright refrain,
While solar flares can't hide their pain.
"It's too hot!" the Earthlings shout,
As sunshine dances all about.

Moonlight giggles on tranquil seas,
While meteors buzz like bumblebees.
Every night they start their flight,
Chasing dreams with sheer delight.

Stars tell tales of ancient lore,
Of space pirates and alien folk galore.
They're plotting pranks on distant suns,
Whispering laughter that never runs.

Galaxies whirl in a lovely spin,
Sassy clusters packed with grins.
In the universe's wide embrace,
A party waits in endless space.

Celestial Imprints on the Fabric of Time

Time is a fabric woven tight,
Each atom twinkles, oh what a sight!
Stars tick-tock, not missing a beat,
As galaxies cha-cha, oh so sweet.

Black holes play hide and seek, it's true,
Gobbling light when they feel blue.
While wormholes giggle, spinning fast,
Warping moments, oh what a blast!

Calendars float on waves of space,
With a doodle, they sketch each place.
'A birthday party!' the stardust cries,
With cake made of light that never dies.

So join this dance beneath the stars,
Forget your worries, drop your jars.
In this realm where laughter shines,
We're all linked in silly lines.

When Dreams Collide with the Cosmos

A dreamer once flew to the moon,
With a sandwich tucked tight, humming a tune.
The stars laughed as he tripped on a star,
Said, 'Next time, buddy, don't sleep in your car!'

He met a green alien named Clyde,
Who claimed he could teach him how to glide.
They danced on the rings of Saturn so bright,
But tripped over comets in sheer delight!

Clyde served up space juice, quite a delight,
Made of stardust and giggles, a true sight.
They toasted to dreams they'd never quite find,
Laughter echoing through voids unconfined.

When morning came, back down he would land,
With memories tangled like cosmic strands.
He chuckled, "What a journey, oh so absurd!
I'll stick to my couch, that sounds less blurred!"

Light Years and Heartbeats

In a spaceship powered by pizza and cheer,
Zippy the cat flew without any fear.
She counted her heartbeats, one, two, then three,
"Does this count as my cardio? Let's wait and see!"

The stars winked and giggled with radiant beams,
As Zippy declared she was chasing her dreams.
She danced with a comet named Fluffy McFlare,
"Let's race to the edges, if you dare!"

Past Jupiter's moons, oh, the sprinkling lights,
Zippy tossed confetti, igniting the nights.
"Who knew the universe could be this much fun?"
She laughed with the planets as they started to run!

With a flip and a twirl, they spun through the dark,
Stumbling on stardust, leaving a spark.
When she finally landed, her heart all aglow,
She said, "Intergalactic adventures, more please, let's go!"

A Voyage through Time and Starlight

Captain Blip took a wild space ride,
With his robot pal, named Wobble McGuide.
They zoomed past the past and spun through the haze,
Playing tag with history in comical ways.

"Um, Wobble, what's that?" said Captain Blip,
Pointing at a dino with a spaceship dip.
"Just a T-Rex who's learning to fly!
Careful, or he might take you up high!"

Through ancient times, they pirouetted in glee,
Swinging through eras like they were on a spree.
With laughter and giggles, they left trails behind,
As knights played hopscotch, and pirates unwind.

When they hit the stop button, history turned,
"I need a vacation!" the captain yearned.
But Wobble just winked, and with circuits all bright,
"Let's make a new era, full of fun and delight!"

Whirling Gases and Cosmic Tales

In a nebula vast, where colors unfold,
Lived a bunch of gas clouds, both silly and bold.
They swapped twinkling stories of stars made of cheese,
While bouncing on moons like kids on the breeze.

One cloud named Bert declared, "Let's play a game!
Who can spiral the most without going lame?"
So they whirled and they twirled in a dizzying chase,
Leaving a trail of giggles and bright glowing grace.

They juggled little meteors, round like a ball,
While singing a song about the fate of it all.
"Who needs a plan when you can just float?
We'll make up our rules, on giggle we'll dote!"

As dawn peeked in, with light o'er the scene,
The clouds all agreed, "We're the funny routine!"
With laughter that echoed through the void in delight,
They promised to meet every starry night.

Moonsong Mosaic

In a dance of cheese and stars,
The moon wears sunglasses, oh, so bizarre!
She winks at Earth, a playful tease,
Making tides giggle with the breeze.

Planets giggle in their orbits wide,
While asteroids play tag, and can't decide.
A comet's got a tail like cotton candy,
Zooming past where it gets quite dandy.

Saturn's rings are a hula hoop's song,
Encouraging all that dance along.
With each twirl, as laughter explodes,
Galaxies stumble down glittery roads.

So raise a glass to the starry night,
Where laughter echoes, taking flight.
In this universe, we jest and play,
Making memories that never decay.

Comet's Trail

A comet zooms with a fruity scent,
Leaving behind a fizzy trail, heaven-sent.
It sneezes stardust on all who stare,
And giggles while giving an interstellar glare.

Asteroids throw a rock concert loud,
While Mars tries to draw in a celestial crowd.
Venus dresses in glittering sprays,
As intergalactic parties unfold in arrays.

Black holes are just vacuum cleaners, you see,
Sucking in all like a cosmic spree.
While satellites spy from their lofty perch,
Data reports on the galactic church.

So let's ride along on this comet's flight,
With snacks of stardust, we'll feast tonight.
As we sail through the skies full of cheer,
In this universe, we'll spread joy and beer!

Andromeda's Adoration

In Andromeda, where we play dress-up,
Stars wear tiaras, and space cats sup.
Sharing tales of moons that lost their way,
While aliens dance the night away.

Shooting stars throw a surprise parade,
With confetti made from cosmic fade.
Galaxies gossip about twinkling sights,
As planets exchange their curious bites.

Nebulae swirl like fluffs of cotton,
Creating patterns that leave us begotten.
Eclipses giggle, peeking and hiding,
While comets declare a reign of gliding.

So grab your rainbow space shoes tight,
And dance with the stars, oh what a sight!
In this galaxy of giggles and dreams,
We'll toast to the fun, or so it seems.

Quantum Quatrains

In quantum realms, where jesters grin,
Particles prance in a mischievous spin.
Quarks play hopscotch, giggling away,
As we wonder just how they play.

Wormholes loop like ribbons in the breeze,
Sending time on hilarious teas.
Photons chuckle in their light-speed quest,
While gravity trips on its own silly jest.

Supernovae burst with a fireworks cheer,
While space-time stretches, wanting a beer.
In this universe, where chaos roams free,
Nothing's absurd when it's funny, you see!

So let's dance in a quantum delight,
With laughter exploding far into the night.
Where science meets chuckles, we'll spin and twirl,
In the fabric of space, let's give it a whirl.

Stardust Serenade

Twinkling lights in a salad bowl,
Aliens dance on a giant roll.
With each twirl, they spill some beans,
Cosmic chaos in shiny jeans.

Asteroids join in a silly race,
While comets wear a silly face.
They giggle and bounce, what a sight,
Throwing star confetti at night!

Planets wobble to a funky beat,
Dancing in circles with two left feet.
While Saturn's rings harmonize,
A melody that tickles the skies.

So grab your hat, take a flight,
Join the fun and dance tonight!
The universe sings a happy tune,
Under the silver, winking moon.

Celestial Echoes

Jupiter's donuts cause quite a fuss,
Ringed with icing, they make a big plus.
Saturn's moons field a wacky game,
With outer space jokes, all the same.

Black holes slurp like a cosmic shake,
While shooting stars giggle and quake.
Astro-nuts swing on stellar vines,
Cracking up over space-time signs.

In the Milky Way, the cows all fly,
Mooing in harmony with a cosmic sigh.
Galaxies spin, so wild and free,
Sipping on stardust, just like me!

With laughter echoing through the void,
The universe is never devoid.
Join the fun, elevate your cheer,
For space is a party, year after year.

Lunar Lullabies

On a crescent moon, a cat takes a seat,
Chasing moonbeams on tiny feet.
Stars are snoring in pajamas bright,
As comets giggle with all their might.

Night's a playground with space bunnies,
Hopping 'round in their cute, fluffy tummies.
They pull pranks that float in the air,
Nibbling on cheese, without a care.

The sun hides behind a fluffy cloud,
Making the stars feel extra proud.
In this laughing galaxy, all feels right,
Even the black holes smile tonight.

So sing along with celestial charms,
Dance under the glow, as the cosmos swarms.
With sweet dreams wrapped in twinkling rays,
Lunar lullabies ignite the fays.

Nebula's Whisper

A purple cloud whispers silly tales,
Of space pirates with rainbow trails.
They steal ice cream from a comet's cart,
Waging battles with jellybeans for art.

Meteor showers rain candy treats,
While planets twirl in their funny beats.
Astrological jokes fill the air,
As stars share secrets without a care.

Galactic giggles float far and wide,
With aliens slipping in for a ride.
They swing from the tails of cosmic kites,
Spreading laughter, oh what delights!

So if you hear the nebula sigh,
Join in the fun, don't be shy!
With every whisper, joy ignites,
In the vastness where laughter lights.

The Sound of Starlight

Whispers from the moon, so bright,
They tickle my ears, what a sight!
Stars giggle and dance in the dark,
While comets play tag, leaving a spark.

Planets all gather, sharing a joke,
While Saturn spins rings, oh what a bloke!
Mars tells tall tales of Martian delight,
As Venus just winks, oh what a night!

Black holes chuckle, pulling you in,
With gravity's charm, they're sure to win!
Asteroids laugh, dodging a fuss,
While space dust just floats, who's got the bus?

Nebulas puff clouds, so fluffy and grand,
Each one a painter, with colors at hand.
In this silly expanse, so vast and so wide,
Even the stars can't help but glide!

Twilight Tales

When twilight whispers the day's last call,
Stars spin stories, oh one and all!
The sun takes a nap, tucked under the sea,
While owls crack jokes, just you and me.

The milky way swirls, like a creamy delight,
With sprinkles of stardust, oh what a sight!
Fireflies join in, with their glowing dance,
Creating a scene that makes us all prance.

Night critters gather, each one a delight,
Telling their tales by the pale moonlight.
The wise old crickets, they chirp with glee,
As the shadows just chuckle under the tree.

So hold onto tight, this whimsical night,
For laughter's in stardust, sparkling bright!
Let the rhythm of twilight keep your heart warm,
As laughter and joy become nature's charm!

Spiral Galaxy Serenade

In the spiral's embrace, we twirl like a tune,
Dancing to echoes of the dreamy moon!
Galaxies giggle, swirling 'round fast,
While black holes just grunt, "This spinning won't last!"

Stars are the backup, singing away,
While planets get dizzy, in their own ballet!
Comets come whizzing, put on a show,
With tails like confetti, they steal the glow.

Aliens peek from their ships, taking a seat,
Laughing aloud at this cosmic retreat.
They sip on stardust, munch on moon pies,
As they watch the galaxy do its surprise.

With laughter and joy in this spiral affair,
Each twinkle a chuckle, without a care.
So let's whirl together around and around,
In this joyous expanse, wonder is found!

Celestial Cartographer

A map of the heavens, I sketch with delight,
Pinpoints of laughter, twinkling so bright!
The Milky Way's streamers, I follow with glee,
Drawing odd shapes that just look like me!

Planets parade in a line so absurd,
Venus tripping over, haven't you heard?
Mercury zooms, oh what a deer,
While Neptune just giggles, "This way, my dear!"

Stars wear their hats, they sway on a breeze,
As meteors race off, striking poses with ease.
And here comes a UFO, zooming so fast,
With an alien driver, having a blast!

So join in my quest, let's map the bizarre,
With giggles and grins, we'll reach for that star!
In the universe's dance, let your heart roam,
For every sketch leads us closer to home!

www.ingramcontent.com/pod-product-compliance
Lightning Source LLC
Chambersburg PA
CBHW072145200426
43209CB00051B/563